Jackie Robinson

by Karen English
illustrated by Dan Brown

McGraw-Hill School Division
New York Farmington

When Jackie Robinson hit his first home run for the Dodgers, none of his teammates shook his hand. A black man had never played on a major league baseball team before Jackie. Some white Americans wanted to keep it that way.

Jackie knew African Americans could play as well as anyone else.

Playing well was easy for Jackie. But he knew that playing well while people called him names would be very hard.

Jackie was used to being disliked because of his skin color. He was born in Georgia. At that time, blacks and whites in Georgia didn't go to school together. They didn't even sit in the same part of the bus.

Then Jackie's family moved to California. Life was still hard. But things were better there.

Jackie became good at many sports. Many people accepted him because of that.

Jackie was so good at sports that a school in California paid all his college costs. The school wanted Jackie to play on its teams.

After college and the army, Jackie played baseball on an all-black team. Branch Rickey saw him play. Rickey worked for a major league team called the Brooklyn Dodgers. He could use good black players on his team.

Branch Rickey knew Jackie could play well. He also believed Jackie was a strong person. He would have to be strong to face the hard times ahead.

Rickey talked to Jackie about playing for the Dodgers. Jackie was surprised. He thought Rickey wanted him for a Negro league.

Rickey asked Jackie hard questions. Could he stay calm if people called him names? Could he look away if they threw things?

"I'm looking for a man with the guts not to fight back," he told Jackie.

Jackie told Branch Rickey he could do it.

But he didn't know how hard it would be. He had always stood up for himself. Now he would have to keep quiet. But Jackie had to do this. He wanted to help other African Americans get into the major leagues.

Other players didn't like Branch Rickey's plan. Even some Dodgers were mad. They said they would not play on a team with a black man. But Branch Rickey did not back down. Neither did Jackie Robinson.

In the end, the Dodgers said they would play. So did the other teams. But they showed their anger in other ways. Pitchers threw balls too close to Jackie's head. Runners would slide into him.

Sometimes Jackie wanted to fight back. But he knew he couldn't. That would only make it harder for other black players to be hired.

Sometimes, getting angry made Jackie play even better.

Soon, Jackie's teammates grew to respect his great talents. Time after time, he helped them win.

Jackie Robinson played with the Dodgers for ten years. He helped them win the 1955 World Series. He was a great ball player. He was also a great hero in the fight for the rights of African Americans.